SECULAR

SATB and piano

OXFORD

Two Elizabethan Lyrics

Robert A. Harris

MUSIC DEPARTMENT

OXFORD
UNIVERSITY PRESS

Two Elizabethan Lyrics was commissioned by Keynote Arts Associates, James Dash, President, for the Chicago Choral Festival. The composer conducted the first performances on 28 and 29 April 1990.

Although the commission stipulated a work for chorus and orchestra, *Two Elizabethan Lyrics* may also be performed with the piano accompaniment provided in this score.

Instrumentation

2 Flutes	2 Bassoons
2 Oboes	2 Horns in F
2 Clarinets in B♭	Strings

Orchestral score and parts are available on rental from the publisher.

Duration
About 10 minutes

TWO ELIZABETHAN LYRICS

ROBERT A. HARRIS

1. The Passionate Shepherd to his Love

Christopher Marlowe (1564–1593)

4

love,   And we will all   the

love,   And we will all   the

love,   And we will all   the

love,   And we will all   the

pleas - dim. - ures prove.*

pleas - ures prove.*

pleas - ures prove.*

pleas - ures prove.*

* Prove: to try or experience.

6

Slowing   [35] rit. poco a tempo

And all the crag - gy moun - tains — yields.

hills, — and fields,   And all the crag - gy moun - tains — yields.

And all the crag - gy moun -tains — yields.

hills, — and fields,   And all the crag - gy— moun - tains yields.

8

40 Simply and gently (♩=60-63)

And we will sit upon the rocks, See-ing the shep-herds

And we will sit up-on the rocks, See-ing the shep-herds

And we will sit upon the rocks, See-ing the shep-herds

And we will sit up-on the rocks, See-ing the shep-herds

40 Simply and gently (♩=60-63)

45

feed their flocks, By shal-low riv-ers to whose

feed their flocks,

feed their flocks, By shal-low riv-ers to whose

feed their flocks,

45

10

*kirtle: a robe

14

16

18

2. The Nymph's Reply to the Shepherd

Sir Walter Raleigh (1552–1618)

*Philomel: the nightingale

24

28

*Date: ending

Two Elizabethan Lyrics HARRIS

OXFORD
UNIVERSITY PRESS

www.oup.com

ISBN 978-0-19-385856-5

9 780193 858565